Little BIG Horns

by Robert R. O'Brien
illustrated by Michael Digiorgio

Harcourt

Orlando   Boston   Dallas   Chicago   San Diego

Visit *The Learning Site!*

www.harcourtschool.com

SPRING

It is lambing time for the bighorns. Many of the ewes have already left the flock. They stay away for a few days. They find a quiet place away from the other sheep. In this place, they have their babies.

After the babies are born, the ewes return to the flock. Their little lambs follow them. They wobble on their thin little legs, but they must follow their mothers.

The lambs stay close to their mothers. They nurse often, gaining strength from the sweet milk.

One ewe looks for a safe place away from the flock. She sees the high meadows above her. In a few weeks, she will lead her lamb up the mountains. They will feed on the abundant grasses in the high meadows.

For now, she has to find a safe place to have her lamb. She wanders for a while. She finds a good spot, only to discover that another sheep is having her lamb there.

Finally, she finds a gully with no other sheep around. She stays there and waits for her baby to be born.

Surprise! There are two lambs. They are beautiful. Their little horns are nubs. They kneel on the grass, blinking their eyes. Sometimes they cry piteously until they find their mother.

The mother is tired from giving birth. Still, she does not dare surrender to sleep. She must watch for danger. Her lambs are weak and helpless, easy prey for an eagle or bobcat. Coyotes, and even bears, sometimes take newborn lambs. She must protect them. She must stay awake.

A few days pass, and the lambs start to gain strength in their legs. Though they are small, they are already jumping a little bit. Their legs get stronger with each jump.

The mother and her lambs are bonding with each other. The mother gives them lots of attention. They are brother and sister.

They know that they belong together. The sister is the older one. She was born first, but she is just slightly smaller. The brother's legs have a harder job because they support a larger body. He stumbles more than his sister.

After a week, the mother lamb returns to the flock. There are three other mothers and their lambs.

The flock also has some young rams that are not fully grown. One older ram is the leader of the flock. He will lead the flock up the mountainside in a few weeks.

For now, the sheep stay where they are. They graze, letting the lambs grow stronger. The lambs play and jump around. The twins have been jumping since barely two weeks after their birth. Sometimes one of the ewes watches another ewe's lamb along with her own.

SUMMER

It is time to move the lambs up to the alpine meadows. Now they are big enough to make the trip. The lead ram guides the way uphill. The rest of the flock follow him.

A ram from another flock stands in front of them. He faces the lead ram. He eyes the flock and snorts. He challenges the lead ram of the flock.

The lead ram snorts and paws the ground. He lowers his head. The other ram does the same. Suddenly they leap forward, charging towards each other. Who will win?

There is a loud CRACK of horn upon horn. They hit head to head. They back up and charge each other again.

The valley below echoes with the sound of their battle. Again and again they charge. They fill the air with the noise of their horns crashing against each other. It seems impossible that either ram could survive such a violent contest.

Finally, the battle ceases. The lead ram has won. He has kept control of his flock. The other ram turns and walks off. The flock moves around nervously.

The lead ram was not injured in the fight. The other ram was not hurt either. The fight was to show which ram was stronger. The ewes need a strong ram to follow. They need a strong ram to help them defend the lambs from lynx and eagles.

After a few moments, the lead ram walks
up the mountain. His flock quickly follows him.
The mountain valley is quiet again.

Now it is high summer. The sheep have found a meadow where they can graze. The young twins jump and bounce and chase each other. They have grown in size. They have grown in skills. They can run and jump almost as well as their mother.

Their mother is still on the lookout for danger. Now the sheep have an advantage. Bighorn sheep have very good eyesight. In the meadows on the hillsides, they can see far away. The slightest movement puts them on alert. At the first sign of trouble, they run. The sheep can bound quickly up rocky slopes. They can go where no predator can catch them.

One of the reasons the mother has to be so alert is that the young rams have all left the flock. They have gone to other pastures. They gather in small groups and graze separately from the ewes.

The young rams in each group put themselves in order from the most important to the least important. The most important rams are usually the ones with the biggest horns. They get to choose their own flock of ewes. If two rams have nearly the same size horns, they may fight. Rams are rarely injured in these fights.

FALL

Summer changes to fall. The coats of the bighorn sheep change. They become a rich brown. The weather turns cooler. The younger rams start to drift back to the flocks.

One day, the lambs are playing and jumping. They take turns playing what looks like "follow the leader." Each of the lambs tries to outdo the other.

One of the twins makes a daring jump. He jumps onto a rock ledge. His sister, not to be outdone, jumps up, too. She joins him on the ledge. None of the others follow. There is a good reason. They have all bounded away.

They have spotted a lynx. The rest of the flock
has leaped up the rocky paths. No other animal
has the ability to climb these paths. The twins
are trapped on their ledge. There is a high wall
behind them. They can't jump up. If they move,
the lynx will see them.

   The twins stand still. The lynx has seen them.
He picks his way through the rocks. He is trying
to get as close as he can. The twins are paralyzed
with fear.

Suddenly the lambs see a movement down below them. The lynx hears a sound. It is their mother! The lynx turns to face the ewe. He is confused. He can handle one of the lambs, but he's not sure about this ewe. He looks from the ewe below to the twins above. He seems to be trying to decide which animal to attack.

Suddenly the decision is made for him. A dark shape hurtles down the hillside, bounding over the rocks. It is the ram!

He charges fearlessly toward the lynx. The lynx doesn't have to think twice. He turns around and runs, going as fast as he can.

The ewe comes to the bottom of the ledge. She bleats to tell the lambs it's all right to come down. The male wiggles and fidgets. He is not sure he can make the jump.

The young female leaps off the ledge. She picks her way through the rocks to her mother. The male sees that it can be done. He jumps off the ledge a few moments later.

The rest of the sheep come down from their hiding places. The lynx is gone. The first snowflakes begin to fall. Winter is coming.

WINTER

Now snow has covered most of the sheep's summer grazing grounds. The bighorn sheep head toward fields that face south. They find grazing places where the snow cover is thin.

After a while they move down to the tundra. There they sometimes have to share their grazing area with elk and deer. There may be domestic sheep there, too. Domestic sheep have woolly coats and no horns.

Next spring the twins will be bigger and stronger. They will be fast runners, able to care for themselves. They will return with the flock to the rocky mountainside of their first summer. Next spring there will be new lambs to join the flock.